California
The Golden Coast

California
The Golden Coast

text by Philip L. Fradkin

photographs by Dennis Stock

A Studio Book · THE VIKING PRESS · New York

For Alex, my companion
P.L.F.

For Ed and Peggy Wayburn,
who have done so much for us all.
D.S.

Contents

The North Coast

There is no mistaking where the California coastline begins. The traveler on U.S. Highway 101—two lanes here but a freeway by the time it reaches the Mexican border more than a thousand miles distant—leaves Oregon behind just after the Winchuck River. On the right is an agricultural inspection station. These stations are placed at every major road entry into the state to filter out dangers to livestock and crops and to warn the traveler that he is entering a different land.

Despite urbanization in the nation's most populated state, agriculture—termed agri-business to include related services—is the biggest industry, and land is the most important commodity. Nowhere is land more sought after than along the coastline, where agriculture is a dying art but recreation, commerce, tourism, industry, and the pursuit of the Good Life are booming. This is land to be bought, sold, traded, and held for speculation. It is land to be drilled, graded, paved, furrowed, and trod upon by millions who want to work and play here where the continent ends in unequaled splendor.

And it all begins a few feet over the border. A sign on the ocean side of the highway declares, "Development opportunities. 112 acres. Motel sites. Commercial sites. Homes sites. Private airstrip." A little farther away a companion sign reads, "No trespassing. Violators will be prosecuted." Both themes are to be repeated with little variation and increasing tempo on the journey south into People Land.

But here, far enough away from the large urban centers, a great deal of natural beauty remains. On this day, ignoring the signs, I turned off the paved highway and drove to the edge of the Pacific Ocean. It was one of those vivid early-fall days. A thin sliver of fog hung far out over the horizon. Each form was sharply edged. It was a world of fresh greens, of blues fringed by a dazzling white surf line and the complementary grays of weathered driftwood and beach sand. Farther south the tones become more muted—shading to the more representative California hues of olive-green vegetation, soft yellow grasses, the burnt orange of the sun, brown soils, and the gray veil of fog—but here on this day there was an aching intensity of light and color.

The north coast, from the Oregon border to San Francisco, is bucolic California. The low coastal hills are lush with second-growth timber. Here, in a near rain-forest climate, there can be up to one hundred inches of rainfall a year. Small ranches roll gently up the slopes while offshore a few guano-splattered rocks show where the powerful ocean swells have beaten back the headlands to form Pelican State Beach.

The winter storms flush out the coastal hillsides and rivers, disgorging limbs, logs, and miscellaneous debris onto the beaches. These piles of wild forms rest above the high-tide mark until they are plucked by another storm to again journey down the coast. Pelican Beach is littered with this driftwood, bleached to a color that begs to be caressed. It is a place where a child's imagination runs wild and an adult seeks meaning in forms and comfort in texture.

It is a tranquil, warm day. A hawk and a few gulls circle slowly, the perennial hunt. The swordlike dune grass sways softly. Above, on a bluff, is the Smith River Indian Reservation, a few dilapidated shacks and the How-On-Quet Cemetery overlooking the beach. Plastic flowers add splashes of unreal color to the carefully tended graves, and a weathered picket fence keeps out encroaching sand dunes.

8

The grandest tombstone of all belongs to Mattie Richards—June 14, 1922–September 21, 1970, "Beloved wife and mother."

A few miles to the south, a fisherman clad in hip boots sits on a bench overlooking the Smith River and laments, "Not much luck here now. We need a rain to raise the level of the river so the salmon can go up and spawn."

The man is older, probably retired. He wears a yachtsman's cap and on the sleeve of his brown windbreaker there is a National Rifle Association patch. Definitely a sportsman. The man continues, "I'm from Salinas. But I like it here better. I like to see some trees and shrubs and grass and to walk on the ground."

The traveler is now firmly into California, where almost everybody at one time or another seeks his place on the coastline.

The forces of nature can be brutal on the north coast. Although most of the state is disaster prone—fires, earthquakes, landslides, mudslides, snowslides, and floods —it is only in the north that storms reach truly epic proportions. Elsewhere disasters occur wherever man has overbuilt on a fragile land.

Nowhere is the violence of storms more evident than along St. George Reef, a series of nine visible rocks and uncounted underwater ledges stretching 6½ miles northwest from the rounded, treeless bluffs of Point St. George. Northwest Seal Rock is farthest out, and in a gray tower, 146 feet above sea level, is the beacon of the lighthouse.

Jonathan Rock is 3⅕ miles southwest of this light. Deep water surrounds this slight protrusion and breakers warn of its existence only in a heavy swell. The overcrowded coastal steamer *Brother Jonathan* was trying to make the safety of nearby Crescent City harbor in June 1865, when her boilers failed to provide the needed thrust to overcome the waves spawned by a northwest gale and she was swept onto Jonathan Rock. The ship was quickly pounded to pieces and only 19 of the 232 passengers aboard survived.

There was a public outcry about maritime safety that reached back to the halls of Congress but it was not until 1891, when the lighthouse went into operation, that the forces of nature and government inertia were finally overcome. The story of its construction was an incessant duel with nature.

Because of rough weather, only three landings were made on Northwest Seal Rock in 1882, when a preliminary lighthouse survey was made. Since the rock was only above water twice a day during high tide, construction supplies and the workers could not be housed on the rock. The steamship *Alliance* was leased as both a floating home and a supply barge. It broke away from its moorings the first time it was anchored off the rock.

The workmen commuted to their jobs via a breeches buoy slung from the ship's mast to a ring bolt drilled in the rock. A half dozen men rode in a cage from the ship to the rock—a trip which took three minutes and sometimes resulted in a dunking when the cable went slack. When the tide rose, the men lashed their tools to the rock and made for the ship.

In the winter of 1883 a series of severe storms swept the rock. All work ceased while the workmen watched boulders weighing at least ten tons being tossed around like golf balls. The herculean task dragged on year after year as Congress failed to appropriate enough money to complete the job.

The fortress against the sea, with cut granite stones weighing up to seventeen tons lining its walls, was finally completed twenty-six years after the *Brother Jonathan* sank. In 1923 huge seas from a winter storm smashed an iron platform seventy feet above sea level. In 1952 the three lighthouse keepers and twelve additional coastguardsmen were marooned on the rock for twelve days by a storm. A relief lighthouse crew landed, but a new storm arose and all were trapped. Waves from this storm broke over the 134-foot structure and a few panes of glass sheltering the lantern were shattered.

St. George Reef is not the only notorious graveyard of ships along this rocky coastline which offers few harbors of refuge and is storm-lashed or cloaked in fog for much of the year.

To the south and 185 miles north of San Francisco is Cape Mendocino, the farthest westward point of land in the contiguous United States. As at Point Conception in southern California, coastal shipping has to make a course adjustment here. The headland was used as a landfall by the Manila galleons of the Spanish who first spotted land here in 1565, on the long voyage from the Philippines to Acapulco, Mexico. Upon sighting the rolling, grass-covered hillsides sliced by deep ravines, the treasure-loaded galleons altered course to the south. Spain's interest in the California coastline stemmed from a desire to protect this lucrative trade.

There are major weather changes to the north and south of the cape here, as there are at Point Conception. There is more fog and the prevailing northwest winds blow less violently to the south of the cape. Rainfall is greater north of the barrier. Concerning the cape, the navigator's Bible, the *Coast Pilot,* warns, "In view of the dangers in the vicinity, it should be approached with considerable caution in thick weather."

The rocks off the cape have accounted for more than two hundred shipwrecks since 1850. Blunts Reef extends nearly three miles out from the cape and consists of two small black rocks about 230 feet apart. They are awash and clearly visible. The Blunts Reef Lightship, with its red hull, now stands guard over this danger, and "Blunts" is marked in large white letters on its side.

But on Friday, January 6, 1860, there was no lightship and seemingly little need for one in the light rain and calm seas. The steamship *Northerner* was plodding along at a steady twelve knots on her way to Portland, Oregon, and Vancouver and Victoria in British Columbia, Canada. The ship never reached its destinations. It struck Blunts Reef and, like a wounded animal, blundered 4½ miles further north to a death in the surf at Centerville Beach. There a white-concrete cross marks the sinking.

Captain William L. Dall, one of the survivors, published a note of thanks in the *Humboldt Times* to the people of the area for the help they rendered the survivors. But not all of the good citizens of Humboldt County acted with a Christian conscience. Looting of goods that washed ashore was widespread and some persons were unconscionably charged for voluntary services. The newspaper caustically noted, "Many reasonable bills were paid. For instance, one man whose calling is to save souls charged the modest sum of five dollars for saving a life. He, too, was paid."

The coast was to claim many more lives down through the years. The most common fear now of the numerous pleasure-boat owners is being sliced in two while in the steamer lanes. The one-hundred-foot motor yacht *Morning Star* was sunk by a freighter in the fall of 1972 off Cape Mendocino and two small children were lost in the seas.

For eighteen days the freighter *Liberty Manufacturer* was a neighbor of mine while it rested on the rocks off Point Fermin near the entrance to Los Angeles harbor that same fall. In the confusion of a shipboard fight the vessel passed on the wrong side of a buoy while turning back to port. It provided a great spectacle for a large metropolitan area before it was dragged off the rocks by a salvage tug. Carelessness and the raw forces of nature are the major causes of shipwrecks on a coast that forgives little.

Coastal fogs are the curse of summertime tourists–the knowledgeable natives know better and travel in the uncrowded, bright fall months—but without these cool mists California would shrivel up under the relentless hot sun and there would be no redwood trees. This would not only be an economic and aesthetic loss, it would be a spiritual deprival as well. The redwoods, extending from just north of the Oregon border to the Big Sur coastline below Monterey, are nurtured on the fogs, which contribute an additional thirty to forty inches of needed moisture in the dry months.

So many writers have described the world's tallest trees in terms of church architecture and religiosity that one hesitates to do so again. But it is true. The venerable silence of a redwood grove extends vertically, and the visitor's spirit is compelled to reach up while his feet remain rooted in the rich humus below. I suppose sugar-plum fairies or nasty satyrs, as well as a Bach fugue, might also travel along the transparent shafts of light filtered through the foliage from far above. But the feeling that always comes to me in these groves is one of soaring toward a higher existence.

The 58,000-acre Redwood National Park runs for thirty-three miles along the north coast south of Crescent City—if one is sharp enough to spot the signs and find the way toward the few facilities the park offers. Born out of the conflicting desires of lumbermen and conservationists, the park is now a neglected child as is another recent creation of the National Park System to the south, Point Reyes National Seashore. It was a lot easier to carve national parks out of existing federal lands in the 1800s that it is to reach the sometimes hollow, hard-fought compromises of these years. A Congress that likes to pat itself on the back as a proud father yet will not provide child support is also no help.

The logging trucks still roll inside the Redwood National Park boundaries, bravely dedicated a half dozen years ago by Lady Bird Johnson in what now seems like that naïve era of beautification. The lumber companies are cutting timber right up to the borders of the park, and this does little for the pristine scenery not to mention the resulting siltation of the streams within the park. Two of the most interesting areas in the park are outside the control of the Park Service. They are the mouth of the Klamath River, owned privately and by the state, and Prairie Creek State Park.

During the height of the fall salmon season one of those mass recreation scenes for which the state is so justly famous takes place at the mouth of the Klamath, one of the last free-flowing rivers in California. Thousands of fishermen line the sand spit, jostling, bumping, sometimes hitting and climbing over each other for a chance to catch one of the hundreds of king and silver salmon or steelhead trout that migrate up the river, providing they can swim by this human wall.

With an outgoing current from a falling tide, an interesting scene develops.

Should a motor on one of the boats conk out, it would be dragged by the swift current into the breaking surf. So a Coast Guard dory plays sheep dog, flitting about at the head of the flock to intercept any disabled boat. The action resembles that of a lithe ballet dancer prancing in front of an elephantine chorus.

On shore, friends and relatives gather about driftwood fires awaiting the return of the meat hunters. Should there be success, it would be followed by a feast accompanied by the tribal rites of beer drinking and sounds of muted revelry. House trailers, campers, and motor homes—symbols of middle-class, outdoor America—are parked bumper-to-bumper. There is shelter from the biting northwest wind and all the comforts of home, including television.

On the same day a different scene is unfolding a few miles to the south—on Gold Bluffs Beach within Prairie Creek State Park. Although the foothills of the Sierra Nevada are better known for producing gold, two years after the 1849 gold rush miners were also swarming over the north coast to search for the precious metal. They found very little but there were enough disappointed miners to settle the area. The sands of the beach were worked for gold and then abandoned after a short time.

The rounded bluffs are dull yellow and on this evening they were enlivened by a brilliant setting sun. A mellow gold was reflected everywhere—on the green fringe of firs and pines along the tops of the bluffs, in the sands of the dunes stretching to the beach, and on the small, rounded pebbles washed clean by the surf at the edge of the ocean.

About a hundred yards from where I was camped with my six-year-old son, two bull Roosevelt elk engaged in a stylized combat. They did not seek blood, but rather form. We remained silent—no small feat for my son—as we continued to eat our dinner. The scenery and entertainment were unexcelled.

The two elk stood still for minutes, then faced each other. Slowly they interlocked horns, and then their dark brown necks strained. It seemed as if they were arm wrestling, elk style. They would wrestle their horns to one side or the other, then back off and engage each other again. The perfect red disk of a sun, radiating

14

intense heat at the edges, set below the horizon and a cool land breeze sprang up. The two elk lost interest in their mock combat and wandered off to the main herd, which moved slowly into the dark woods for the night. For some reason I felt that the Orient was very close in that serene hour.

The next morning my son and I found the elk herd grazing in a small meadow atop the bluffs. The indentations of their bodies were still outlined in the wet meadow grass, showing where they had slept. We had reached the small glade from the dark grotto of Fern Canyon. The sandstone bluffs have been eroded away by the waters of Home Creek, leaving sixty-foot-high vertical walls densely matted with ferns above a wide, flat creek bed.

Within moments after entering the U-shaped canyon the sound of surf vanishes. To walk through the canyon is like swimming through an underwater garden. Water drips through the thick moss and the rich profusion of ferns—five-finger, lady, sword, deer, leather, bracken, and chain ferns. Decaying tree trunks have toppled into the canyon. Insects dash madly about in the early morning shafts of light, creating intense activity in an otherwise still place, secret and moist like a body cavity within the earth.

The problem with writing about the California coastline is that to do it right and with enjoyment you have to write about those places that have meaning. For me, such places are the remote ones. They are not the tourist traps of Mendocino, Monterey, Big Sur, and Laguna Beach, or the quiet ostentatious atmosphere of such well-off seaside living areas as Sea Ranch, Carmel, and Newport Beach. Equally uninteresting are the less palatial areas, the wall-to-wall housing of Pacifica and Oceanside. A port has meaning, so does coastal agriculture—they fit and seem real. But other industrial developments such as oil wells and power plants, although grudgingly necessary, are ugly intrusions.

The places that have the greatest meaning to me along the coastline are where the feeling of timelessness—the rhythmic eternity of waves beating against a headland, or winds and rains molding rounded hills and carving steep canyons—dominate the more temporal works of man. The problem of writing about such places is that they then do not remain untouched for long.

One such place is the fifty-five-mile stretch of virtually untouched coast from Centerville to Cottoneva Creek three miles north of Rockport. Since these are near-nonexistent geographical locators south of Eureka and the Eel River valley, there is some chance the area will not be quickly found. Here, without coastal highway or railroad tracks, is the longest stretch of virgin shoreline in the state. One paved road traverses four miles of the coast in the northern portion of this forgotten area. At about the halfway point another road slices in from the interior to bisect the coast at Shelter Cove. Roads have been laid out over the hillsides here but few homes have been built in the planned recreational subdivision, which has become a modern ghost town. The area is wilderness invaded by only a few one-lane dirt roads used mostly by hunters and ranchers. That such a large area could still exist unspoiled is a tribute to the public's dependence on large Detroit-built automobiles that cannot hack the rutted lanes.

My son and I camped at the mouth of the Mattole River, where oil was first drilled in the state and was shipped in 1865 from the aptly named town of Petrolia. There were none of those tract-sized campsites found in state and national parks. The space was open with plenty of driftwood to use for a fire on the sand spit lying between the ocean and the lagoon. The pond of fresh water was formed by the lethargic summertime river, which will burst through the fragile sand barrier during the first heavy winter rains to repeat a cycle of rejuvenation.

Wild, yes; remote, also true. But we had a neighbor on the beach who fit the scene. His name was Dan. I don't know his last name; to ask would have been an unnecessary intrusion. We met Dan when my car became stuck in the sand. I had seen his driftwood enclosure, and not wanting to impose on his privacy, I sought a camping spot about a half mile distant. In the process the car bogged down. So I walked over to Dan's shelter to ask for help and we became acquainted.

16

Later, Dan, with his gentle manner, charmed my small son, Alex, by showing off his proudest possessions—a mongrel dog named Stoney and her nine tiny puppies. Stoney let Alex fondle the puppies in the small windbreak Dan had built for her comfort.

Above Dan's home flew two unusual banners. He explained that Japanese mothers believe the symbols of carp give strength to their sons. That night Stoney got her strength, which I suppose she did pass on to her sons, from a large hunk of sausage I left out untended.

Dan smoked a corncob pipe and read books on mysticism. He seemed to be about forty-five, and he indicated that he had been a businessman in the South. Starting in Mexico, Dan had followed an unnamed quest along the coastline to the mouth of the Mattole River. He had found what he wanted there and was going no further. The first project that Dan had in mind was to build a sweatbath on the beach. Then he wanted to buy some land a little farther back and build a more permanent hut modeled after the homes of Mongolian sheepherders. In the few months Dan had been there, he had gotten along well with the local ranchers, who usually distrust strangers. Maybe they sensed Dan fit the land. Like the bleached driftwood, which matched the color of his hair, he had come to rest above the mean high-tide mark.

For all his sense of adventure, Dan had not traversed the wild coastline to the south, having heard that automobiles would have difficulty there. The unknown drew us, so we left the next day. From this point on the King Range National Conservation Area begins to unfold. Many people, including the poet Robinson Jeffers, celebrated the easily accessible coastline around Big Sur, but if they had made the trek here they would have found equal if not greater splendors. The huge flanks of mountains, dappled with golden grasslands and fringed by deep woods, tumble steeply down four thousand feet to the ocean. There is an immediacy between the mountains and the sea found in few other places.

The Bureau of Land Management, an arm of the Department of the Interior, has placed a sign at the crest of the range. It reads, "Pacific Coast Primitive Area. The public lands on the Pacific Coast have been designated for preservation and protection in their natural condition." Up from the wooded ridge goes the winding trail, finally emerging at the 4087-foot top of Kings Peak, the highest mountain in the range. The blast of wind forces a group of hikers to bend over; violent fits and starts rake the bare summit and the bowed shrubbery just below the crest. About ten miles off a coastal freighter heads north, also contending with the wind. The white froth of surf beats on massive headlands as far as the eye can see in both directions. Below us, the silver ribbon of a creek emerges from a wooded canyon to disgorge its contents into the ocean. Hereabouts there are still mountain lions and black bears. Stand quietly and feel that sense of timelessness.

The history of the north coast is written in the number of trees cut to satisfy the building needs of cities to the south and across the nation. The massive timber harvest of redwood and Douglas fir was one of those periodic economic convulsions in the state that irretrievably altered the face of the land. First it was the widespread grazing of cattle and sheep, dating from the time of the Spaniards. This changed the grasses from perennials to annuals. Then it was gold, and the devastating results of hydraulic mining and mining by dredge can be seen to this day in the Mother Lode communities along the foothills of the Sierra Nevada. Next was timber on the north coast, followed by the draining of mountain streams to make the desert bloom. Since World War II, urbanization has added asphalt, concrete, cinder block, and stucco to the landscape.

The timber industry, like agriculture, is dying along the coast. Too many trees have been cut and the second growth has not reached maturity. The loggers have gone inland in search of more trees. But such "doghole ports" as Rockport once were booming towns. Now they are skeletons of the past. Grass is growing tall in the yard of the boarded-up school, and the swing rusts in the playground. The row houses of the company town have been devoured by the vegetation, a tribute to the

18

great regenerative qualities of the land. There now are a half dozen residents where once Rockport throbbed with the lives and activities of eight hundred.

A doghole port had barely enough room for a dog to turn around, so the saying went. Any slight indentation in the coast would do. In the 1880s at the height of the lumber boom there were seventy-six such ports from Bodega Head, north of San Francisco, to Eureka. The only qualifications were enough deep water near shore and some protection from the prevailing northwest wind and waves. Lumber was loaded from shore by ingeniously designed wooden chutes or by wires stretched from land to the vessel.

The lucrative trade spawned the last of the nation's great sailing fleets. More than five hundred wooden sailing vessels were built on the Pacific Coast between 1860 and 1905, and some continued in use up to 1950. The West Coasters at first were two-masted schooners. Later they grew to be four- and five-masters, only to be replaced around the turn of the century by steam-powered schooners. The specifications for the ships remained the same: they were built to be worked in and out of small ports by a few sailors, to carry tremendous loads, and to beat into the prevailing northwesterlies without ballast.

Rockport had a chute and a 250-foot-long wire suspension bridge connecting the mainland to a flat rock offshore where the lumber was loaded onto the schooners. The pilings for the bridge remain today at the northern end of the small, rocky bight. As a doghole, Rockport was regarded as dangerous. In 1892 the steam schooner *Venture* was wrecked there and five of her crew drowned while loading lumber. A sudden storm descended on the exposed anchorage, the mooring parted, and the ship could not get up headway quickly enough to avoid the rocks.

Rockport's economic ups and downs began when a sawmill was built in 1877. The owner, Dudley R. Miller, sold out to the Cottoneva Lumber Co. in the depression year of 1887. Cottoneva closed down operations in 1910. Then, in 1925, one of the strangest lumber industry operations in the West began when the Finkbine-Guild Lumber Co. of Jackson, Mississippi, took over.

What was at the time the tremendous amount of $1.5 million was poured into constructing a company town. The paternalistic firm built more than a hundred homes, a hotel, a company store, and a new mill to replace the one previously destroyed by fire. Instead of sawing logs into lumber, the mill turned out cants, squared-off logs that were shipped to Mississippi to be sawed into planks. It took the company two years to go broke under this arrangement. Its operations were finally discontinued in 1929, another depression year.

The Rockport Redwood Co. bought the town and the remaining timber in 1938 and continued milling operations until 1957, when the lack of redwood and Douglas fir made it necessary to manage the land as a "tree farm," a logging company euphemism meaning there is little or nothing left to cut. Yet the land is resilient. One day it may grow back to supply again the needs of a boom-or-bust lumber economy.

Some old lumber towns die and stay dead, decaying ghosts of past glories, while others are resurrected to lead different lives. Since Mendocino was the first town on the north coast, one would expect it to also be the deadest. Instead, it is alive and thriving as a tourist attraction and art colony, spectacularly set on a bleak headland. Its stark New-England-style architecture has survived virtually intact from the mid-1800s.

In California age is an oddity and Mendocino is considered venerable. It dates from 1852 when one of seven Chinese junks bound for California was shipwrecked nearby. A salvage crew arrived from San Francisco and the riches they found were not silks, teas, or opium but the soaring redwoods. Word got back that year to "Honest" Harry Meiggs, described as one of the biggest swindlers of the San Francisco gold rush era, and he soon arrived on the scene to build a mill at the mouth of Big River. Two years later he hastily departed with his partners' funds for South America, where he continued to make money building a railroad over the Andes. Meiggsville then became Mendocino.

The town boomed with the heavy demand for lumber. In its heyday it could boast of twenty-one saloons and eight hotels. For those who did not want to drink, there was the Mendocino Hotel, known as the Temperance House. The hotel and many of the other original structures, including the Masonic Hall with its picturesque redwood carving of "Father Time and the Beautiful Maiden" atop a cupola, still stand.

As in other doghole ports along the coast, the lumber schooners were sometimes trapped by storms and flung against the rocks near town. A publication of the Mendocino County Historical Society states as true the story that a sailing vessel disappeared with all on board into a blowhole south of the mouth of Big River. A young mother aboard another ship, seeing that she faced a similar fate, secured her baby to a chopping bowl and dropped the wooden implement into the bay. The baby was rescued and a Mrs. Spencer Hill cared for it until the grandparents could arrive from Chile.

Mendocino declined as a lumber town during the early part of this century and lay dormant until the 1950s, when artists and beatniks discovered its quaintness. If the visitor walks about town on a quiet day he gets the rare feeling, for California, of being among man-made things that have lasted for a long time. There are the bleached-gray fence stakes covered with velvet lichen, ducks waddling from a pond, the crisp lines of New England architecture, a windmill standing gaunt against the sky, and some picturesque neglect. The movie companies know a good thing. *Johnny Belinda, East of Eden,* and *The Russians Are Coming, the Russians Are Coming* were all filmed here.

There are two areas of outstanding natural beauty near Mendocino. One starts on the now vacant flat where Harry Meiggs built his mill more than a hundred years ago. I wanted to explore it. I put my son between my legs, a friend climbed into the front seat of my two-man kayak, and we paddled up Big River and back into time. A short distance in from the flats at the river's mouth the hills begin to impinge on either side. There is still logging done in the Mendocino area by the present owners of the timberland, Boise Cascade Corp., and as we paddled quietly a chain saw and tractor shattered the silence on the south bank. My friend asked, "Isn't there some substitute for wood?" I could think of no answer.

After a few curves Big River, which really is not very big but is larger than the nearby Little River, straightens out for a quarter mile or so. Floating on an old log boom near the north bank was a small cottage with smoke curling from its chimney. Inside on this fog-chilled day was a bearded man reading a book by a lamp. It was a warm sight as we passed noiselessly by.

The kayak, the least obtrusive vessel I know, served as a sort of snow plow by pushing the wildlife ahead of its progress. We caught up to a blue heron and then a snowy white egret. They flew ahead three or four hundred yards and then awaited our approach to repeat their futile, evasive movements. Soon we encountered eight small ducks who were on the verge of flying but just couldn't quite make it. They would splash madly ahead and then await our coming. The mother, meanwhile, would fly by with gusto and a great many quacks and then circle quietly back when she saw we hadn't been diverted. Then, again, the mad scramble upriver, to my son's delight. The ducklings must have been tiring. After the sixth or seventh futile dash, the brood remained stock still until we drew abreast and then there was a mad scramble downstream and to safety. The transparent maneuvers lacked cunning.

Further upstream the river narrowed and there was a log barrier to negotiate. An otter slipped noiselessly into the water and disappeared from sight, a much more effective escape than any other wildlife had executed that day. The undergrowth was dense and the coastal fog gave way to dappled sunlight filtered through the canopy of second-growth trees.

It was time to eat lunch so I beached the kayak on a sandbar next to some stout pilings that had once supported the trestle of a logging railroad. Vines had crawled up pilings, which no longer supported anything, and redwood timbers marched irregularly into the thick undergrowth. My son made a make-believe fort out of driftwood at the base of the pilings. I was reminded of the columns of an ancient temple being reclaimed by the jungle. I suppose the answer to my friend would have been that given time, the land will erase man's mark.

The other beautiful area is nearby Russian Gulch State Park, where I have had good days skin diving for abalone and sitting on headlands, which resemble Japanese prints in their softly textured, linear quality, watching the surf surge through the rocks where I had been diving. There are wind-bent Mendocino cypress trees on the fingerlike headlands. A short distance inland it suddenly becomes very quiet. The deep forest of redwood, western hemlock, tan oak, and California laurel is carpeted with ferns that crowd the small brooks glittering over black rocks. It is surprising how quickly the vast ocean can be lost a few steps inland.

There is also a small forest near Mendocino. In this pigmy forest the trees are dwarfed because of the highly acidic condition of the soil. I once went to a fair at a hippie commune here. Along the forest trails there were blankets spread with jewelry, leatherwork, candles, and beads—all haphazardly displayed. There was also a jar of free cookies. People ambled about, talked, smoked marijuana, ate popcorn, and stretched out in the sun-warmed grass to hear a fine string quartet. It was all very improbable—a hippie fair in the pigmy forest with classical accompaniment—but in Mendocino it worked.

It is a lonely land, described in books as being solemn, an island in time. Point Reyes is the only sweeping cape along the California coast, the others being mere blemishes on a pockmarked face. It juts out into a cold, misty Pacific Ocean with a bloated fishhook shape. It is only thirty miles north of San Francisco, yet it is isolated from the urban scene by the lack of fast roads, a dismal climate, and the great sheer of the San Andreas Fault. During the 1906 earthquake that devastated San Francisco, land on the west side of the fault moved north twenty-one feet in the Point Reyes area. The fault, visible along the eastern edge of the peninsula, is not so much a physical barrier as a clear line of demarcation heralding the fact that something separate is about to occur on the other side.

Point Reyes is a National Seashore administered by the Park Service, the first such federal land unit on the West Coast. There are still privately owned ranches within the seashore's boundaries, but dairy farming is a compatible land use in what is essentially a pastoral scene. Even after the Seashore was created in 1962 by President John F. Kennedy, the subdividers and loggers threatened to desecrate it. Finally, with enough money appropriated by Congress, those threats were beaten back. Now Point Reyes is a relatively undisturbed meeting place of flora and fauna from the north and south.

The incredible diversity of life is striking. The average annual rainfall at the tip of the point is 11.6 inches, 1.6 inches more than the limit that qualifies an area for desert status. Yet inland the average rainfall is over 30 inches, enough to support deep forests and moist grottoes. More than three hundred species of birds range over the shore and seventy-two species of mammals have been recorded here.

The rich profusion of forms starts at the edge of the sea in the intertidal zone where life was first spawned. Here, living in rhythm with the tides and withstanding the power of the surf yet deriving sustenance from it, are all the myriad, multi-colored forms of tidepool life. Beds of sea lettuce are green. There are purple sea urchins and the sun's rays filter through the swaying stems of brown kelps—the redwoods of the sea floor. To dive into the subtidal zone is to surrender to the rhythmic sweep of the current rushing between rocky outcrops. The thick seaweeds, hiding such delicious treasures as lobster and abalone, stream by in graceful arcs.

On the beach are the shore birds and offshore, gliding with barely a motion inside the curl of a large breaker, are brown pelicans, birds whose ugliness in repose is redeemed by their fluid grace in flight. Less venturesome and more land-prone are such birds as the marbled godwit and the long-billed curlew, whose long beaks probe for food the casual observer would never suspect existed below the sand. The small sanderlings collect in busy groups and move about, in and out, feeding at the edge of the surf line. It is hard to believe that these seemingly mindless creatures are capable of migrating from the Arctic to the Southern Hemisphere.

Offshore, the gray whale can be seen migrating from the Bering Sea to Scammons Lagoon in Baja California.

Above the stretches of intermittent sand and rocks are the cliffs and bluffs, the dominant feature of the North and Central coasts. In the far south there are long, sandy beaches, but here the coastline is young, most of it still in the process of being upthrust, and little has been eroded. The California coast has a dramatic, movable quality. It seems to be always in motion, mirroring the restlessness of the inhabitants along the shoreline. The bluffs are mostly composed of sandstone. They lack the substantialness of granite and are more easily eroded into weird and dramatic forms. Combined with the numerous earthquake faults that traverse this edge of the Pacific "rim of fire," there is a feeling of fragility, of temporariness—an awareness that it could all slip into the sea during some cataclysmic event.

The hills just above the bluffs are mostly treeless, swept by strong salt-laden winds. Only coastal shrubs interspersed with grasslands, golden in the summer and greened by winter rains, survive here. The aromatic oils of the shrubbery, the sage-brush and lavender, give these areas a perfumed fragrance. The eucalyptus trees have a more pungent smell. There are also salmonberry, thimbleberry, and black-berry along with shrubby lupine and bush monkeyflower on these gentle slopes. Further back, taller and more impenetrable, is the chaparral—brittle, prickly, and more drought-resistant. Feeding on the explosive oils within these shrubs, fires can ravage coastal hillsides at tremendous speeds.

From this dry, crinkly environment a visitor may suddenly find himself plunged into the lushness of a canyon-button forest of coast live oak, California laurel, dogwood, willow, and alder. These communities of lesser trees sometimes signal the nearby presence of a redwood grove or a stand of Douglas fir if there is enough rainfall and fog—conditions that can vary within a few hundred feet.

The bald hillsides along the coast are ideal grazing land for beef and dairy cattle which, along with sheep, have devastated some portions of these ranch lands by overgrazing. With its protective cover gone, the topsoil washes away, leaving a barren landscape. Mice are busy tunneling under the dry grasses. Hawks circle above on invisible air currents looking for prey. The coyotes and gray foxes are out competing for food, too. There are ground squirrels and chipmunks scampering about. A mule deer moves with ease from the brush to the forest. At night the owls, skunks, and racoons take over. The wildlife is abundant. In the warmer, dryer sections of the coastline there are rattlesnakes, but the greatest danger I have ever encountered is poison oak and barbed-wire fences.

The Central Coast

It may be because of the winds and the chilling fog, or perhaps it is because growth first centered around the commercial aspects of a fine harbor, but San Francisco spreads inland around the bay rather than laterally up or down the coastline. North of the Golden Gate Bridge the affluent suburbs of Marin County can barely be detected from the ocean; they are clustered on the balmy side of the coastal hills. South from San Francisco, a sharply etched alabaster city from the water, the view is much the same except for the short stretch to Pacifica. Here, within the space of a few miles, is the counterpart of the dense tract developments in southern California that northerners like to mock.

But the bluffs dotted with monotonously designed homes soon drop off to the fertile agricultural fields of the Half Moon Bay area. A few miles farther south, where San Mateo and Santa Cruz counties meet, is Ano Nuevo State Preserve. The preserve is a peculiarity along this section of the coast, barely noticeable and hardly visited by the three million or so people who live in the nearby San Francisco Bay Area.

Maybe this is because there is no sign advertising its existence a short distance off the coastal highway or because it has gotten little public attention for its low-keyed attractions. There is also, for some, the problem of having to walk. The preserve consists of a dirt parking lot and trails leading over plowed fields to a wind-protected beach and a desolate point. It is the combination of small things that makes Ano Nuevo a pleasure to visit.

Agriculture reaches its most intensive development along the central coast, but it is in a state of decline here as elsewhere on a shoreline that has become a hot real-estate property. Farmhouses and barns are plastered with "for sale" signs or left to gracefully rot into the ground. Repairs on ranch buildings are minimal and it is difficult to find a new barn. Increasing residential demand—particularly for the ubiquitous second home or for recreational subdivisions—has forced the value of the land to rise and property taxes are taking a larger bite out of farm incomes. The inevitable result is a sellout to developers.

Within a few years, California's brussel sprout production, 88 per cent of the nation's total and almost all of it located near here, will be nonexistent. Artichoke fields to the south of Santa Cruz are endangered, as are cattle-grazing lands. The coastal agriculture is only a small portion of what goes on statewide but if the land has to be productively used, farming is one of the more pleasant ways.

The plowed fields extend right to the edge of the bluff, where there is a sharp drop to the beach lying in the lee of Point Ano Nuevo. There are surfers at the western edge of the beach on this day, gracefully threading their way through breakers against the backdrop of a sculptured yellow sandstone cliff. It is our first indication of the near fetish of the south—contact with sun and surf.

Now the pleasant surprises begin. A short distance offshore outcrops of the same sandstone assume the shapes of a submarine or a miniature Matterhorn on which the droppings of the resting black cormorants form a snowy summit. The sand dunes, ridged with parallel ripples unmarked by human feet, start here and lead out to the point. Mystery surrounds the skeletal remains of the abandoned light-house buildings on an offshore islet. The barking of hundreds of seals and sea lions emerge out of the fog from this low rocky promontory.

While this tiny island is barred to all but qualified researchers, I once wandered among thousands of seals and sea lions on a long sand spit at the northwest end of desolate San Miguel Island, one of the Channel Islands to the south. There I encountered the world's ugliest animal—the shuffling, sluglike bull elephant seal. He is the largest of the pinnipeds and is distinguished by a pendulous snout extending below the chin. Combined with the rolls of fat around his neck, enough to make the stoutest dowager look sleek by comparison, and two tons of bulk packed within a sixteen-foot frame, it makes him difficult to match for sheer nonbeauty.

Hundreds of thousands of elephant seals were killed in the 1800s for the oil that was rendered from their blubber. Whales encountered a similar fate. By 1869 the seals were virtually extinct and so rare that they were not worth harvesting. There was a single herd of less than one hundred on the island of Guadalupe off Baja California. The number began to increase in the early 1900s. At present it is estimated that the seals, now protected by law, are about thirty thousand. There are some bright spots in the environmental status of coastal wildlife. Not only is the elephant-seal population up, but sea otters and brown pelicans—also once thought extinct—are making strong comebacks.

The sex life of a bull elephant seal on Ano Nuevo, as documented by researchers, is the height of male chauvinism. The reigning bulls do not court the females, who are conveniently arranged in harems, but rather they physically subdue them in a clumsy rape scene. First the big bull bites the female on the back of the neck—a gesture of affection similar to being caressed by the jaws of a steam shovel—then he drops the full weight of his body, perhaps four thousand pounds, on the lady's back and pins her down.

The bull's whole life is directed toward this one act. It is rarely consummated because he has to fight off competing males, who use the slightest indiscretion and resulting inattention to personal defense as a chance to take advantage of their foe. Social rank is dependent on the ability to dominate the females, who have no choice in the matter and are utterly promiscuous. Who gets the females is determined by bloody battles lasting as long as forty-five minutes.

These fights among the lumbering slugs have all the mystique of primeval combat. They start with the bull throwing his head back and warning his opponent with a series of low-pitched, pulsing sounds. Then with surprising agility the bulls move into close quarters. Standing chest-to-chest, with fully one-half of their torsos extended upward, they seek with feints and strikes to sink their teeth into each other's thick necks. This is all for the sake of a female who is probably being tackled by a third bull that sneaked into the harem while the other two were beating their chests.

As Ano Nuevo is rarely visited, so has the stretch of coastline from Monterey to Big Sur become touristville. And rightly so. There are all the necessary ingredients. Monterey, the old Spanish capital of California, is where European man's history of this state and the West Coast began. Many of the old adobe buildings, dating back to the late 1700s, are still standing in this preservationist-minded area.

This is a monied stretch of coastline—both in terms of its permanent residents and the life-styles they have adopted and in what is offered the tourist. There are shops—mostly in what I think of as the "shoppe" style—to tempt buyers in Monterey and Carmel, whose once-sleepy charm has taken on a pretentious quaintness. For creature comforts there are luxurious hotels and gabled rooming houses, expensive restaurants in subdued settings or the more honky-tonk atmosphere of Fisherman's Wharf in Monterey. For the athletically inclined there are scores of tennis courts and a tennis ranch along with some of the finest golf courses in the world. This is where Bing Crosby has his annual clambake, a pro-amateur golf tournament. For entertainment there are folk and jazz festivals and the setting sun.

The Monterey peninsula and the wilder area from Carmel south to Big Sur have never needed a chamber of commerce to promote their glories. Well-known writers, artists, and photographers have provided this service free of charge. Robert Louis Stevenson, who drew on this area for descriptive scenes in *Treasure Island*, started it all off in 1880 when he wrote, "On no other coast that I know shall you enjoy, in calm, sunny weather, such a spectacle of Ocean's greatness, such beauty of changing colour, or such degrees of thunder in the sound. The very air is more than usually salty by this Homeric deep." Stevenson knew the area well enough to qualify his praise with the word "sunny." The frequent summer fogs tend to limit the vistas.

John Steinbeck drew on some of the most pungent, earthy aspects of life on Cannery Row in Monterey. His description in *Tortilla Flat* of fog in a coastal forest, perhaps that of nearby Point Lobos, is one of the best I know. The poet Robinson Jeffers had a more Olympian view and treated the Big Sur country as a setting for a Greek tragedy. Henry Miller led a quiet life in Big Sur after World War II, but nevertheless his presence gave the area its freewheeling bohemian reputation simply by implication, as a result of the content of his works. This attracted such beat generation writers as Jack Kerouac, and that in turn influenced the hippy invasion of the late 1960s. The photographers Edward Weston and Ansel Adams found elemental forms here in the dramatic meeting of land and sea.

This unintended promotional influence of the writer and the artist, an influence some later came to regret when they began to lose their privacy, has its most visible manifestation along Cannery Row today. The Row has been sanitized with fancy restaurants, bars, a discotheque and shops from what Steinbeck described nearly forty years ago as "a poem, a stink, a grating noise, a quality of light, a tone, a habit, a nostalgia, a dream." The Row declined when the sardines began to disappear in the late 1940s and it grew deserted and quiet except for occasional fires. Now, in rejuvenated buildings, it has a new life due entirely to its earlier immortalization.

There is a Steinbeck Movie Theater—playing *The Hot Rock* when I last visited the Row—and a bust of the author with the above quotation in front of a parking lot. The Lee Chong Market now calls itself The Old General Store and sells antiques and Steinbeck's books. The La Ida Café is an expensive restaurant and Flora's Whiskey Saloon serves both sandwiches and Mace Franklin at the piano bar Monday through Saturday. Dancers gyrate to rock music below garishly painted boilers in a discotheque that fails to faithfully reproduce the sweatshop conditions of the old canneries. There is one reminder of the more individual, noncommercial past. Scrawled high atop one building in blue paint is the message, "I love you baby blue."

From the frivolity of Cannery Row the coastline enters the sedate community of Pacific Grove, where the streets are dotted with ornate Victorian-style homes and marked by the quietness that comes to a town whose roots go back to a strict Methodist past. Molest a butterfly in this town and it is a misdemeanor. Monarch butterflies are so important in Pacific Grove because they return from as far as three thousand miles away to nest in their favorite trees.

The sedateness continues through Pebble Beach and the 17-Mile Drive but it is more hidden here—hidden behind the gates of large estates, pseudo castles, and large one-story ranch-style homes of the retired and rich who have sought seclusion ever since Andrew Carnegie arrived a century ago in his private railroad car. Adjacent Carmel has a sparkling, white-sand beach and more of those shoppes. It also has a well-preserved reminder of the Spanish heritage—the serene Mission San Carlos Borromeo, one of the twenty-one missions founded in California by the intrepid priest-explorer Father Junipero Serra, who is buried in the Carmel Mission.

Father Serra established the mission in 1770 at the same time that secular authorities were setting up the Presidio in nearby Monterey to protect Spain's interests in the newer world. In 1769 Don Gaspar de Portola, the governor of California, came looking for Monterey, which had been described as a sheltered harbor by Sebastian Vizcaino, who explored the coast in 1602. Actually, it was an open roadstead, so Portola did not recognize the site. Instead he planted a wooden cross on a knoll beside the mouth of the Carmel River a few miles away. In 1770, returning by foot from San Diego, he had better luck and found Monterey.

A replica of that cross stands on an unmarked knoll with a 360-degree view. In spring the hillock is bedecked with wild flowers and the aromatic smell of the coastal chapparal. Just south are the contoured streets of a modern subdivision, and above are the textured hills marking the start of the Santa Lucia Range. Continuing in an arc to the east are abandoned artichoke fields. They have been proposed for development but are being desperately sought by Carmel citizens who are trying to raise money to preserve the coastal plain as open space. Beyond in the flat of the Carmel Valley is a shopping center, and to the north are hillside homes secluded by trees. On the beach are sunbathers and skin divers in black-rubber wet suits. Children are playing in the calm river waters. California has come a long way since Portola's day, but just a little west of south is the ragged outline of Point Lobos, looking much as it did those two hundred years ago.

Point Lobos is perhaps the most spectacular bit of land along the California coastline. I say perhaps, because on any given day my mood can change. It depends on where I am, since memory is short and I am greatly influenced by the immediacy of beauty. Nearby Big Sur is more massive, Point Reyes is more brooding, Russian Gulch more textured, and Prairie Creek more varied. The fifty-five-mile stretch of coast in the north is wilder, and the five northernmost Channel Islands off southern California are more remote.

But Point Lobos, a 1250-acre state preserve, is a finer, more fragile, almost feminine piece of serrated land, yet it is deceptively strong. On summer weekends it can be crowded but this too can be considered a plus, for the still remaining abundance of wildlife then seems all the more remarkable. It was on this point, on a crowded Saturday, that I saw—at the same time—the fine vapor spouts and glistening black backs of a pod of gray whales migrating north, sea lions resting on Sea Lion Rocks, and in a kelp bed below me three sea otters cavorting amidst the twisting vines.

While the marine life is abundant and the granite cliffs are spectacularly indented, the point is most noted for its trees. As the redwood in its sheltered grove rams its way skyward with ruler straightness, so does the Monterey cypress bend and contort itself to escape the full brunt of the winds. The strength of these prevailing northwest winds can be measured in the difficulty that was encountered here in erecting a lighthouse at sea, by the numerous shipwrecks or by the adaptive forces that nature has gathered along the coast to evade their punishment. It was almost as if the land itself was tilted to offer the least resistance to the swells rolling in unobstructed from mainland Russia and Alaska. The waves, spawned far off by the wind, slide southeast along the nearly parallel coast.

Only at such insolent headlands as Point Lobos can these swells get a firm grip on the land. And it is here under these harsh conditions that the Monterey cypress, native only to this one small area, thrives. A combination of salt spray, fog, and the right soil conditions nurture these relics of a far vaster cypress forest of long ago. These tortured shapes take on an ethereal, unsubstantial quality when the fog descends. They are the shifting dead whose breath comes from dank caves. In these forests the lace-lichen hangs from trees in long folds that feel like cobwebs when they brush against your face.

But the point loses its somberness in the spring when the land comes aflame with carpets of wild flowers. The state flower, the poppy, is the very quintessence of California. It blazes forth in such golden glory that in years past the Spanish called this coast the "Land of Fire." Blue lupine, red Indian paintbrush, purple *Brodiaeas* and mad violets add the exuberance of life to the land.

The sea otters provide a touch of humor as they float on their backs amidst the kelp. They may be grooming themselves or sleeping. With an ingenuity known only to a few other mammals, the otter may be using a flat rock as an anvil on which to crack open an abalone or mussel. Or he may be using the vinelike strands of kelp as an anchor while dozing. In this position he may have a forepaw draped over his eyes to keep out the sunlight. All he needs is a pair of sunglasses to complete the humanlike scene.

The reemergence of the otters is an ecological success story and a tribute to the resilience of these small creatures. They were hunted to near extinction for their pelts, primarily by the Russians who established a permanent colony at Fort Ross north of San Francisco in 1812. The method of hunting varied. Sometimes the animals were surrounded by Aleutian hunters in two-man kayaks, and then the otters were clubbed or speared when they came to the surface for air. At other times the hunters used screaming baby otters as bait. The adults would seek to rescue the youngster and get harpooned in the process. Otters are naturally curious and raise up in the water when they hear a commotion, a trait that enabled them to be shot from shore or from specially designed boats.

In any case it didn't take long to run out of otters, and by 1825 otter hunting was no longer a profitable venture for the Russians, Americans, and British. From 1850 to 1938, when a small group of otters was spotted off the Big Sur coast, they thought to be extinct. The major threat to the otters now comes from oil slicks, which destroy their insulation from the cold waters. A number of otters accidentally drowned their young when they were frightened by a low-flying plane over the preserve that was being used to film *Jonathan Livingston Seagull*. The otters are undoubtedly getting more numerous and the abalone hunters along the central coast claim the otters are destroying this tasty mollusk that is now becoming increasingly rare. The balance of nature swings many ways.

South from Point Lobos, past Carmel Highlands, the Big Sur coastline begins. It stretches seventy-four miles over the torturous, mountainous windings of State Highway 1, with the ocean ever present below. The roadway has been compared in scenic beauty to the Amalfi Drive in Italy and the Grand Corniche on the French Riviera. It is, indeed, awe inspiring.

The road, hewn out of rock by convict laborers who worked roped together on the heights, follows the flanks of the Santa Lucia Mountains that tower four thousand feet above the distant surf. The hillsides can be gently folded, lush with a green-velvet carpet of grass in the spring, or they can be dry with chaparral growth, tumbling quickly down from pine forests on the ridges into moist canyons where redwoods grow and a stream runs all year. Perched here and there, in some of the most improbable places, are homes. Some are ancient ranch houses, others are shacks that housed the convicts, and still more are modern wood and glass aeries. Most of these cannot be seen because the life-style here is very private and the locked gate with the "No trespassing" sign is the firm rule.

And always within sight—except when the fog closes in and the motorist is alone with no other reality than a few feet of undulating road in front—is the ocean that differentiates Big Sur from any other mountain range. From the heights of the roadway the ocean is a rippled, wind-streaked blue expanse with a white fringe of surf nestled against the dark green hills. The wave-mist spewed up by the wind rises as a sort of waterborne smog and lies within the deep indentations. A hawk rides the wind currents. A coastal canyon is spanned by an elegantly arched bridge that echoes the grace of the hawk's flight. And the mountain stream that empties into the ocean carves a serpentine path across the white sands. There is enough repetition of forms to create a massive whole.

Big Sur proper starts where the coastal highway swings inland and encounters the Big Sur River. Before the disastrous 1973 floods the visible community consisted of a few unobtrusive stores, campgrounds, motels, and gas pumps. Much of this was wiped out by the floods that poured through the valley after the fire of the previous fall which denuded the steep hillsides. But the feeling, if not some of the conveniences, of Big Sur remains. It is just a bit more difficult to find a place to spend the night.

Remoteness has historically delayed progress here. The Esselen Indians are the first known inhabitants of the Big Sur area, but the first recorded European visit occurred in 1769 when four members of the Portola expedition were separated from the main group and wandered south. They took eighteen days to hike sixty miles, an approximate daily average of three miles, and finally stumbled exhausted into an Indian encampment at the southern end of the range. In 1834 the Rancho El Sur was created out of a Spanish land grant of twelve thousand acres reaching south from Point Sur. The descendants of the early owners still graze their cattle on these lands. Homesteaders followed and moved up into the valley and out into some of the remote canyons. The numerous grizzly bears, whose form is emblazoned on the state flag but who have long since disappeared from California, preyed on the livestock until a local rancher devised a method of hanging steer fat laced with strychnine from the branches of a tree. Although the road was completed in 1937,

Big Sur remained essentially pastoral. It was still remote enough during World War II to serve as a haven for draft dodgers. After the war came Miller, electricity in 1947, other artists and writers, an art colony, publicity, assorted free souls, miscellaneous affluent escapees, and then tourists.

It was one of those studies that made eminent common sense. The idea was to take a look at the whole Pacific Coast and rate those areas having recreational values. The National Park Service took one year for the job and published its findings in 1959 in a simple but strikingly effective booklet entitled, *Pacific Coast Recreation Survey*. As happens with most studies, nobody paid too much attention to it. That is not too surprising, but what does startle is the fact that conservationists, who are organizationally strong in this state, flouted its recommendations.

One section of the report states, "Point Buchon is a fifteen-mile section of shoreline consisting mainly of exposed rocks, reefs, small coves, prominent points, and overlooks. Many reefs and offshore rocks produce an outstanding display of breakers and surf. This rugged and virtually untouched shoreline has an abundance of marine life in its many tidepools and other marine ecological formations. . . . This large, unspoiled area possesses excellent seashore values and should be acquired for public recreation and conservation of its natural resources." Except for the fifty-five mile stretch of coastline on the North Coast, this area is the only shoreline not traversed by a paved road or railroad.

The northern end near Morro Bay is protected now by Montana de Oro State Park. The name comes from the ranch which used to spread over the hills. It means "mountain of gold," a reference to the spectacular display of spring wild flowers. Much of the state is suffused with a golden color, particularly along the coastline. There is Gold Bluffs Beach in the north, the California poppies, which blaze like fire on Point Lobos, and these hills sweeping upward to fifteen hundred feet and crowned with soft, yellow grasses.

What is most strikingly golden here, however, is the coastal rock formations, layers of marine sedimentary rock uplifted and canted in thin slabs that thrust into the surf like a sinking pile of lumber. To follow the convoluted striations of the bluffs and cliffs is to get an object lesson in the impermanence of the coastline. The fragileness of the rock is accentuated in the place where a blowhole sends ocean spray skyward with a resounding *whoomp* after each wave.

But the bone of contention is not here, it is a few miles south at the point where Diablo Canyon intersects the coast. This land is typical of the central coast, not yet semidesert yet lacking the lush vegetation of the north. It represents an averaging of the whole coast. There is still some running water where a creek tumbles down through Diablo Canyon and over a waterfall to a small fern-lined pool below. There are bishop pine and the coast live oak—a venerable octopus of limbs growing to record diameters here. Historically these hills have been grazing lands for more than a century but recently this was dramatically changed.

At the mouth of the canyon Pacific Gas & Electric Co. has built a nuclear power plant with the permission of the Sierra Club, the largest and one of the most militant national conservation organizations. Both the utility company and the club are headquartered in San Francisco. Club officials now wince at the trade off they accepted that allowed the plant's location in this canyon. Now the club has a blanket policy against coastal siting of any power plant. But there was no such policy in the mid-1960s when the club, fresh from its victories of keeping hydroelectric dams out of the Grand Canyon, was internally torn with dissension over this plant's location.

The giant utility company, the nation's largest private supplier of natural gas and electricity, first sought to put the plant in the Nipomo sand dunes a few miles to the south. The club vigorously opposed this location because the dunes, stretching twelve miles and slowly migrating inland, are unmatched by any similar-sized landform elsewhere on the coast. There had been some oil production in the dunes but not enough to mar their remarkable scenic quality. A large block structure and smokestacks five hundred feet high would have been aesthetically intolerable.

So, without taking a careful look at the remote Diablo Canyon site, after numerous votes by the board of directors and bitterly fought referendums, the Sierra Club decided not to oppose the utility company's plans. The acquiescence was significant because a few years earlier the club had successfully stymied Pacific Gas & Electric's proposed nuclear power plant at Bodega Head, a more visible site north of San Francisco.

Now the plant is built but, like Topsy, the utility company keeps growing and now wants to add additional units. At the same time, the federal government would like to construct a desalinization plant nearby. The transmission lines cut twelve-hundred-foot swaths through the coastal hills and the bare-dirt rights-of-way are clearly visible from the air. It would have been nice to set something aside in this untouched part of the state. The thought was there, if not the deed.

A white wooden cross is supposed to mark the spot but when I was there in the fall of 1972 the small cross on Point Pedernales was reduced to a vertical white stick–hardly suitable to mark the place where the navy lost more ships in ten minutes of peacetime than were lost to enemy action during the whole of World War I. The rusting midsection of a ship now lies at the base of a fifty-foot cliff, the metal no longer stark but softened by time to match the surroundings. The navy probably chooses not to commemorate the disaster that took place here about fifty years ago because it symbolizes the pitfalls of blind, sheeplike obedience to authority —an image the military tries to avoid.

On the fog-shrouded night of September 8, 1923, seven destroyers, in single file, crashed one after the other into the rocks of Point Pedernales, 1½ miles north of Point Arguello. The twelve-mile stretch between Point Arguello and Point Conception is known variously as Cape Horn or Cape Hatteras of the Pacific.

The coastal hills here are low and treeless. The land seems abandoned, a feeling accentuated by the vegetation that has grown over old ranch structures. It is not a pleasant place. I suppose in olden times it would have been suspect as a place where miasmas were afloat, although I saw no coastal bogs. On the day I visited the site the wide paved roads were trafficless. Unusual for a Sunday, but perhaps not, because this area is within Vandenberg Air Force Base, the West Coast equivalent of Cape Kennedy. The sun was neither shining nor was there fog, but a soft mist enveloped the huge missile pads and the electronic paraphernalia on the low ridgelines. Little moved. There was silence. It felt like being suddenly thrust into a scene from a science-fiction thriller in which a deadly poison has been released into the air by a spaceship returning from another planet.

But on that night fifty years ago there was movement. The fourteen ships of Destroyer Squadron Eleven were proceeding at twenty knots from San Francisco to San Diego, testing their engines and engaging in gunnery and tactical exercises along the way. The flagship, the U.S.S. *Delphy*, obtained its bearings from the Point Arguello radio direction finder station and at 2100 hours, 9:00 p.m., the squadron commander, Captain Edward H. Watson, decided that the ship had cleared the point and the course could be changed for an approach into Santa Barbara Channel. He made this decision despite a discrepancy in the radio direction finder and dead reckoning positions.

As the follow-the-leader column swung east onto the new course those on the bridges of the destroyers watched one ship after the other ahead of them disappear into a low, thick fogbank. Five minutes later, still steaming at twenty knots, the *Delphy* struck a rock and was followed in quick succession by the *S. P. Lee, Nicholas, Chauncey, Young, Woodbury,* and *Fuller.*

Secretary of the Navy Edwin Denby found a silver lining in the disaster. He wrote in his annual report that "much good will come. Every officer will study more closely the doctrines of command. He will appreciate more fully his responsibility for the safety of his own ship in time of peace, no matter in what formation steaming or what his general orders may be." And so the navy wiped the seven destroyers from its memory.

San Simeon Bay

Pismo Beach

Big Sur

Oso Flaco

Asilomar

Big Sur

Pelican, Anacapa Islands

Big Sur area

San Pedro

Solvang

La Jolla

Corona del Mar ◄ ►

Santa Monica

Pismo Beach

La Jolla

Marina, Alamito Bay

Coronado

Pelican State Beach

Pebble Beach, near Crescent City

At Prairie Creek State Park

Near Fort Bragg

South of Westport

House near Noyo

Beach below Westport

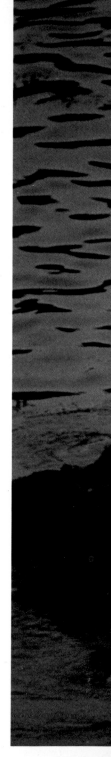

At Salt Point

Bodega Head

Bodega Bay

Smelt fishermen, Wright Beach, Sonoma County

Bolinas Ridge

Valley Ford

Near Mount Tamalpais

Point Reyes

San Francisco

The Golden Gate Bridge

Farms, San Gregorio

Surfing, Ano Nuevo State Reserve

Big Creek, Santa Cruz

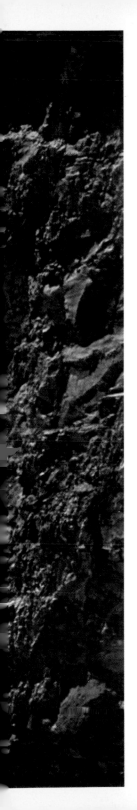

Pacific Grove

◄ ► Hole-in-the-Wall Beach,
north of Santa Cruz

Pismo Beach

Monterey

Big Sur

Point Lobos

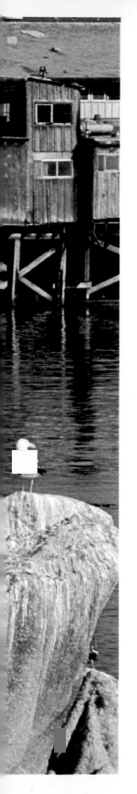

◄ ► Monterey

The South Coast

If you had to balance the coast of California, the fulcrum would probably fall at Point Conception. It lies a little more than two-thirds of the way down the coastline. To the north, with a few exceptions, are areas of great natural beauty. To the south are the people and the works they have created. The California coastline is both of these, mostly in conflict, a few times in harmony.

The Point is a physical barrier. The one time I passed it at sea in a small sailboat it was an utterly calm, moonlit night. There was no wind so the boat's small diesel engine put-putted away. A few lights from ranch buildings twinkled benevolently on shore, and the boat's wake spewed up phosphorescent organisms. The night had a languid, tropical feeling. Yet at other times the tales of the weather off the Point are fearsome.

Here is the mixing bowl of the coastline, where the cold California current sweeps down from Alaska to meet the lesser, warm Davidson current from the south. The result, most of the time, is wind and fogs and the dividing line of the two Californias —north and south. When they speak about splitting the state, this is where the Mason-Dixon line would fall.

Immediately inside the Santa Barbara Channel, in the lee of the Santa Ynez Mountains, the weather can be quite balmy while at the same time, a few miles offshore, a heavy northwest gale can be blowing. Fierce winds sweep down out of the mountains with sudden, devastating force. Fogs can cover the mainland while the Channel Islands to the west are clear, or it can be the other way around or both ways at once.

The coastline does not experience any great climatic changes because of the moderating effect of the ocean currents. They cancel out any great seasonal changes. The sluggish California current, about four hundred miles wide, moves a large body of cold water south. During the spring and summer, when the sun would be expected to be warming inshore waters, the prevailing northwest winds are pushing them steadily south to be displaced by colder subsurface waters. This phenomenon, called upwelling, brings deep, nutrient-rich waters to the surface near shore, thus providing a rich marine life. Warm Pacific air masses blow over the cold inshore waters, and presto—fog. In the fall and early winter the upwelling ceases and the warmer Davidson current takes over, flowing northward up the coast.

Storms are blocked by the relatively stationary Pacific high-pressure area which sits off the coast from April to October. Then it weakens and storms sneak through from the Aleutian low in the winter months, bringing rain along the coast and snow over the interior Sierra Nevada. Unlike the East Coast, the major changes in California weather are from west to east, not north to south.

In the summer months near Point Conception it is not difficult to guess that a major population center lies nearby. To keep out the weekend crowds, the neighboring ranch owner has strung concertina-type barbed wire—particularly effective in trench warfare—partially around his property and employs crewcut guards riding in radio-equipped four-wheel-drive vehicles with German shepherds sitting beside them to keep out the weekend crowds. Surfers circumvent the land-bound guards by arriving in sleek speedboats from as far away as Santa Barbara, forty miles to the east, and anchor offshore. The chase scenes are sometimes worthy of a James Bond thriller.

The intrepid Spanish explorer Juan Rodríguez Cabrillo was the first European to sail up the coast of California, fifty years after Columbus discovered America. Cabrillo was seeking a passage to India and treasure but instead met with death on a barren, wind-swept island. The Spanish were never very lucky in California.

Cabrillo broke his arm on the Isla de Posesion, later renamed San Miguel Island, but his voyage up the stormy coast against the prevailing winds continued. The journal of the voyage provides the earliest recorded description of the coastline.

He may have been in the vicinity of the Big Sur coastline when he wrote, "There are mountains which seem to reach the heavens and the sea beats on them. Sailing along close to land it appears as though they would fall on the ships."

The two small boats were forced back and again landed on San Miguel Island where, on January 3, 1543, Cabrillo died of complications from his arm injury. San Miguel and the other Channel Islands off the crowded coast of southern California have changed little in the last four hundred years. They are long steps back into time. Man's mark is upon them, but not yet with any great degree of permanence.

To walk across San Miguel, the northernmost of the islands, is to feel an unknown presence. It could be Cabrillo or any one of a number of odd, mysterious twists that life has taken on this island. The presences do not start with Cabrillo. They date back at least five thousand and perhaps as far as thirty thousand years when Indians first ranged over the Channel Islands. Access is restricted by the navy so—except for an occasional errant missile which may cause a brush fire—little has disturbed the island.

Jutting out into the cold arctic waters of the California current, Point Bennett, on the northwestern tip of the island, is alive with squirming, prehistoric masses. Up to ten thousand seals and sea lions can be resting on the white sands of the crescent-shaped beach at one time. Walk gingerly among them and you will feel as though you have been thrust into a pit of giant maggots. The tawny brown masses, sleek dark when they emerge from the water, are coated with sand after lying on the beach. They are sprawled over and under each other, sometimes cuddled into tight clusters. There is little regard for daintiness. Flippers are draped over fat guts. Necks arch at the intruder's approach, and dark holes of eyes stare blankly with apparent unconcern—but watch out for that quick lurch.

The way across the island leads up over a gentle shelved slope to an overgrown rutted road used long ago by ranchers and perhaps by the military. The dry, brown headland rises here from the iridescent blue of the ocean water. Spume trails from the many rocks offshore. Up from the grass, which is permanently bent from the force of the winds, jumps a tiny fox, like toast from a toaster. The San Miguel fox is a strange adaptation of a mainland variety; he is smaller because of the harsher environment. He pauses and then darts away when approached. But soon others start popping up along the way.

A grazing herd of brown shapes is spotted across a gentle inland valley that is skirted by the old track. A detour proves they are white-nosed burros. Brought here long ago, they have now grown wild like the pigs, dogs, cats, rabbits, goats, and sheep on some of the other Channel Islands. Of the thirty-four types of mammals found on the islands, fourteen are native to the area and the rest, including a herd of buffalo left on Santa Catalina Island by a movie company, were introduced. And there are eighty plants that are not found elsewhere or are a different type from the mainland variety, which add to the strangeness of the life forms here.

The gently rising track dips now over a series of rolling hills. The island is treeless except for a forest of the past. This copse of low brush is calcified by the salt spray and wind—mummylike forms with contorted limbs wrapped in white shrouds. Top another hill—the highest point on the island is 831 feet—and there are the remains of a wooden antenna forest once used by the military. Rusting cables and other debris lie nearby.

On the descent from the hill the last unsuccessful attempt at ranching on the island can be seen in the ruins of a home. An iron bedstead stands upright amidst the rubble of past lives. A few porcelain bathroom fixtures lie about with unreal whiteness. The story is told of an eastern socialite who found peace ranching with his family on this desolate island but had to be evacuated at the start of World War II. The thought of leaving was too much and he committed suicide. Down the steep canyon from the ruins there is a long, white sandy beach. The water around these offshore islands is a deep indigo color and marvelously clear. Man made one last attempt to occupy Cuyler harbor. The starkly edged ribs of a wooden vessel lie in the shifting sands at the bottom of the cliff.

For the last fifty years there have been proposals to make the five northernmost Channel Islands into a national park. Of the five, three are already owned by the federal government. San Miguel is not accessible but the smaller islands of Anacapa and Santa Barbara are administered by the Park Service as the Channel Islands National Monument. The much larger islands of Santa Cruz and Santa Rosa, which have a greater recreation potential, are privately owned and used for ranching. Of the other offshore islands, Santa Catalina is privately owned and partially developed for the tourist trade, and San Nicolas and San Clemente are controlled by the navy.

The argument against acquiring the five islands for a national park is that dependable transportation from the mainland across the channel is not available, and difficulties could be encountered in the sometimes stormy waters. The private owners have a keen appreciation of the pristine nature of the islands and, except for one oblique threat at subdivision development, have done a better job of preserving the islands than the federal government, which has left its military hardware and other debris lying about. Federal ownership, as has been seen elsewhere along the California coastline, is no guarantee of protection and perhaps—at least for a while —it would be best to keep the recreation-starved public from trampling over these fragile remnants of the past.

A coastline does not exist alone. It is not a detached land form, and is dependent on what happens behind it as well as the more visible, dramatic process of waves sculpturing its façade. On the south coast, man has the largest hand in determining the shape of the coastline and most of his actions have been inadvertent.

It is more than thirty miles to the ocean. There is no water to be seen this time of year in the crackling, dry brushland at the summit of Santa Susana Pass, the dividing line between Los Angeles County and its neighbor to the north, Ventura County. But what begins as a ditch beside the Simi Valley Freeway at the summit of the pass and wends its way through a typical cross section of southern California land ultimately has a very definite effect on a shallow body of water teeming with marine and bird life—the coastal lagoon.

The hillsides here in this early fall month could be aflame in a second, with fire leaping through the explosive chapparal to create one of those periodic infernos for which the area is known. Or, in a flashback scene, cowboy stars of yesteryear might be galloping through those canyons lined with familiar-shaped mushroom rocks where dozens of chases have been filmed. But there are no hoofbeats today, although the freeway hums.

From the ditch, the dry creek bed tumbles westward down the canyon walls while the carefully engineered freeway takes a more circuitous route. The creek skirts a knoll where the Pass Club is perched. "Legal poker and pan. Open to the public seven nights a week. Ladies welcome." And on this weekday afternoon San Fernando Valley housewives with beehive hairdos and tapered slacks are seated about the card tables.

The creek levels out in the Simi Valley and is held within bounds by rock-lined walls, technically called a flood-control channel, as it passes cheek-by-jowl tract houses—the urban spillover from the more crowded San Fernando Valley over the pass to the east. Down again goes the arroyo through Moorpark and past the new college, which has freshly watered green lawns that look unreal in an otherwise arid scene. Below the college is the dusty old town where Mexican movies play on Saturday nights for the farm workers, and cowboy tunes issue forth from the café jukebox.

The "for sale" signs are out on the ranch buildings or tacked to trees. Agriculture in this inland valley is about to give way to suburbs as the pattern of growth from Los Angeles edges into southern Ventura County. But now the land is still pastoral; it is what Los Angeles County was thirty years ago. There are well-tended rows of orange and lemon trees. It is a smogless (although getting less so) Garden of Eden amid the desert wastes.

Near Camarillo the creek passes under Highway 101, now a four-lane freeway. There is a trickle of water in the creek from the treated wastes of a sewer plant and from the runoff of the agricultural fields. When it rains, a torrent rushes past. From Camarillo to the Pacific Coast Highway, the creek bisects the rich, dark earth of Oxnard. Flowing under the highway, its bonds are loosened. The rock walls give way and the creek bed widens into its summation—Point Mugu Lagoon—and the Pacific Ocean.

The lagoon is the last remaining landform of its type that has not been significantly altered in southern California. Along the whole coastline—but particularly on the south coast—such easily filled areas near the ever-desirable water have been the first to yield to housing developments, marinas, and shopping centers. There are now 125,000 acres of wetlands remaining along the coastline, down 67 per cent, or 256,000 acres, from what existed at the turn of the century. These wetlands are essential to the more than one million birds, representing about thirty-five species, which use these marshes when migrating along the Pacific flyway. But birds don't pay taxes to enrich local governments that approve the filling of the wetlands.

The teeming life that exists above and under the waters of Point Mugu Lagoon is as rich and varied as that found in a tropical rain forest. It is still mostly dependent on historic, natural cycles. There are problems, though. Pesticides from agriculture, silt from new construction, and sewage find their way into the lagoon from the creek. Most of this alien material is flushed out by winter rains or the twice daily high tides of ocean water.

The lagoon's complex web of life becomes visible as the waters recede. A white egret stalks slowly through the shallows. A great blue heron rises in alarm, flapping furiously in takeoff but quickly streamlining its form in flight. Brown pelicans rest on the sand spit at the inlet's mouth while a harbor seal pokes his nose above water a short distance away. Most of the life is out of sight, burrowed under the sand. In these hiding places are the food for the birds—mollusks, crabs, echinoderms, and annelids. They rot to form the rich organic material on which later generations of lagoon dwellers will depend for sustenance. Swimming about are top smelt, staghorn sculpin, barred surfperch, and the shovelnose guitarfish.

Into this natural scene the U.S. Army Corps of Engineers would come with a lined flood-control channel. In terms of the current environmental movement, these are the bad guys and this would be a bad idea. But in this case they may be the good guys, since a small part of the lagoon may have to be destroyed in order to save the rest of it.

Allowing nature to follow her course, the lagoon in time would fill up from the materials brought downstream by the creek just as other lagoons farther up the coast have done in recent ages. But then the last good example of this rich form of life would be lost in southern California. So, the thinking goes, halt the natural cycle in place and divert the silt, pesticides, and sewage through a flood-control channel to let the lagoon live—frozen in time.

I live on a bluff overlooking Los Angeles harbor and the ocean. From my window on a clear winter day I can see the snowcapped peak of Mount Baldy where I could be skiing. Below me is the line of breakers on the ocean side of Cabrillo Beach, populated by a few surfers, one or two hardy swimmers, and a few happy wanderers soaking in the aloneness of a winter beach. Whether to climb, ski, sail, or surf; it is one of those California decisions that can tear a person apart—but what a delightful dilemma.

Although I have lived in the Point Fermin area of San Pedro for only slightly over three years, I feel very possessive about it. In a region where so much is homogenized, San Pedro has its own peculiarities and a strong sense of community separatism. Part of this comes from being a port town, a distinction not too many communities can claim and one which has a definite effect. More comes from its varied ethnic mixes.

There are waterfront dives—or there were a lot more before the sterile redevelopment project moved in—Yugoslavian restaurants, Italian and Scandinavian bakeries, corner grocery stores, and a few other amenities that are nonexistent in mile-long shopping centers. It is individualized, still real, and not overrun by tourists as are many other shoreline communities. The scale is close and understandable.

Then there is the beach. Cabrillo Beach is quite unlike any other I have found in the state. In the summer and early fall months it comes alive. It is used. Down from the south-central and eastern portions of the city come the blacks and browns. There is the rich smell of roasting barbecue sauces. Mexican women go wading in their dresses, while small, lithe brown bodies dart about the women's legs. There is the mock scream of a young girl being dragged or carried into the water by young boys who are feeling their male machismo. Their activity is constant—running in and out of the water, throwing and catching, jumping over rocks, or climbing the bluff. Rock music over amplifiers adds an insistent beat.

On most other south coast beaches, the action is languid. Supple young women, inevitably bikini-clad and with long blond hair and bronzed bodies, are the astounding majority, along with their moustached Robert Redford–looking young men. Like feedlot cattle, they seem captives of an exclusive diet—perhaps sun, honey, and milk. They are the epitome of the good health that comes from outdoor living. It is a scene duplicated few other places in the world and it has been celebrated many times in magazines and movies. It is not make-believe. The overall impression on these sun-warmed sands is one of passive surrender of the body. It is an almost compulsive sacrifice of skin, not the vital release that others bring to the edge of the ocean, but rather the seeking of a restorative process—an attempt to heal at the place where life began.

Back at Cabrillo, the blacks are on the concrete fishing pier seriously collecting ingredients for gumbo—fishing isn't a sport here but real meat hunting—and the Orientals are out on the boulder-strewn breakwater gathering up those small creatures and plants, bypassed by others, that have such great potential for the sea-tasting delicacies they create.

There is a funky museum tucked away in the palm trees on the beach with shells and stuffed fish downstairs and ship models and nautical displays upstairs. The amateur collections that make up most of the displays were donated by local inhabitants, adding a personal touch. The polar bears, as the lusty old men who sun and swim year round call themselves, gather nude in the sheltered lee of the men's shower room and talk about their grandchildren and the Old Country. Their younger counterparts, in the search for fit bodies, lift weights next door. It all comes together at the far western end of Los Angeles harbor.

Those who arrived first on the scene did not have many good words to say of the area. To the explorer Juan Rodríguez Cabrillo, the most striking thing about the Los Angeles area in 1542 was the large amount of smoke in the sky, which came from the Indians burning grass to flush out game. He named it Bahia de los Fumos in honor of the smog.

Author Richard Henry Dana, who wrote *Two Years Before the Mast* after he had served as a common seaman for two years, termed San Pedro the worst spot on the coast in 1835, perhaps because two of his shipmates were flogged there, and it was difficult to load hides onto the brig. But Dana indicated its value as a center of commerce. "I also learned, to my surprise, that the desolate-looking place we were in furnished more hides than any port on the coast."

In the late 1800s those large commercial and political forces, which had shaped Los Angeles's growth with such massive projects as the importation of Colorado River and Owens Valley water to the basin, set about getting a first-class port. In 1899 the start was made on what was to become the largest man-made harbor in the Western Hemisphere. When Congress appropriated $3 million to begin building the breakwater, a massive two-day party was held on the bluffs overlooking the tidal flats and parades were staged downtown.

It was civic boosterism at its best. About twenty thousand people arrived at the nonstop picnic to eat 17 head of cattle, 8 hogs, 20 sheep, 3 tons of clams, 2400 loaves of bread, and 250 pounds of coffee. Today it would be impossible even to contemplate such a project on the California coast. It would never survive the effect of an opposing environmental impact statement.

Los Angeles and Long Beach harbors—they are adjacent and compete with each other for the shipping trade—have grown into the center of the state's vast maritime industry, far outstripping San Francisco, which got an early lead during the gold rush. California, whose gross state product is more than that of most nations, is now one of the world's great sea powers. About one-third of the navy's fighting fleet is based in the state. It is home port for about 210 ships and about 170,000 sailors, a total greater than those of all the world's navies except Russia and the United States.

Almost 10 per cent of the nation's foreign trade, imports and exports, flow into and out of the state's major ports. With the rise in popularity of fiberglass boats, southern California, where most of these pleasure craft are made, has become the small-boat capital of the nation. More fish, mostly tuna, are landed in San Pedro than any other port in the nation. The vessels that sail out of San Pedro and San Diego in search of tuna are the last viable remnant of this nation's maritime tradition of men going to sea in small ships to make a living. These modern steel-hulled vessels cruise for months off the coasts of Central and South America where they are sometimes seized and fired upon by Latin nations claiming a two-hundred-mile limit for their territorial seas.

A minor miracle takes place each spring and summer on Cabrillo Beach and certain other beaches extending from north of Point Conception to halfway down the Baja California peninsula. This is the running of the grunion, which occurs at night, when the high tides drive water far up the sand. These small fish, resembling sardines, flop onto the sand in silvery layers just at the moment the tide begins to recede. The female, with a side-to-side motion, digs her way into the sand tailfirst. The male fish, excited by this motion, curls himself around the female. It is a very compassionate scene.

The female lays from one thousand to three thousand pink spherical-shaped eggs and the male emits milt which seeps down into the sand and fertilizes the eggs. Freeing herself from the sand, the female flops back into the water. The whole process takes about thirty seconds. If the eggs escape predators, such as long-beaked shore birds and small children building sand castles, then the next very high tide, in about two weeks' time, will agitate the embryos and out pop the baby grunion, which swim away. I have watched this happening on the beach below where I live against a backdrop of ships gliding in and out of the harbor. Not bad, for city living.

From Santa Barbara south through Los Angeles to San Diego the coastline is almost solidly developed. The people and their homes have crowded impudently right up to, and sometimes over, the breaking waves. The pattern of checkerboard lots is interrupted only by the few coastal lagoons not yet filled and by military reservations that were constructed to implement war but bring peace here to land that is elsewhere being torn apart by bulldozers. Natural values have succumbed to more densely packed homes and higher apartments rising along the balmy, sun-splattered shores. The population is linked to the sea in many ways but in none more devastating and telling than what people have unwittingly done to the *Macrocystis pyrifera,* or giant kelp. The disappearance of the kelp speaks not only for itself but is a harbinger of things to come.

Naturalist Charles Darwin discovered the importance of kelp to the ecosystem 140 years ago during the voyage of the *Beagle* along the western shore of South America. He wrote: "Yet if in any country a forest was destroyed, I do not believe nearly so many species of animals would perish as would here from the destruction of the kelp. Amidst the leaves of this plant numerous species of fish live which nowhere else could find food or shelter; with their destruction the many cormorants and other fishing birds, the otters, seals, and porpoises would soon perish also."

Giant kelp is probably the fastest-growing plant in the world—its rate of growth is about two feet a day. To most people it is just a seaweed, obnoxiously fly-ridden when washed up on the beach. But below the water its majestic vinelike brown tentacles wave sensuously in the current and its blades separate shafts of sun through which large multicolored colonies of fish pass from light into dark shadow.

Attached tenaciously to rocks below, the stems grow to a mature length of one hundred to two hundred feet. Giant kelp is found in this country only along the Pacific coast. It used to grow in great profusion off the south coast but little of it is found today from Malibu to San Diego, a reflection of the growing numbers of people and the wastes they dump into the ocean waters.

The value of kelp is incalculable. There is a tremendous fecundity in these submarine forests immediately noticeable to the diver as he passes from the barren wastelands outside into their vertical life-giving columns. The maze provides hiding places for the deadly moray eel, grotesque sponges, lace-fringed corals, and a multitude of other organisms. The blades are encrusted with tiny sedentary forms, which strain and filter their food from the rich nutrients in the plankton that circulates throughout the area. Other tiny creatures crawl about the stalks, food for the larger fish that graze the kelp. Even man directly benefits. Kelp, when traded on the International Seaweed Exchange, has about three hundred uses in items ranging from vitamins to ice cream to fertilizers.

Enter the villain, the product of a shoddy upbringing. He is the lowly sea urchin; a spiny, prickly creature that thrives on sewage. And, of course, there is a lot of treated sewage dumped into the waters every day off southern California. In addition, the sea urchins' natural enemies are scarce. Elsewhere along the coast the sea otters, who prey on the urchins, are now only beginning to make a reappearance after being hunted to near extinction.

The urchins move slowly along the floor of the ocean, feeding on all forms of vegetation and denuding an area in a way much like that of a plague of locusts. Whole kelp forests have been desecrated. The pattern discovered by researchers at the California Institute of Technology shows that the devastation is greatest nearest sewer outfalls. The sea urchins thrive on the sewage, and the balance of nature has been tipped by man in their favor. The kelp has receded in the face of this vigorous onslaught.

The partial solution that researchers have found is to dump quicklime into the water. This substance is supposedly toxic only to the sea urchins. Scuba-diving clubs have taken a more direct approach with large groups of the divers jumping into the water with hammers to beat back the invaders. Some progress is reported. Areas of kelp are now showing signs of second growth.

The ending, as most true ones are, is rather anticlimactic. It is more a petering out than a grand summation. The natural forces that have shaped the coast are no respecters of international boundaries. The 1,072 miles of the California coastline, whose equivalent length on the east coast would run from Boston to Charleston, ends in a brown semidesert at the Mexican border.

Along the way the sand and rocks, mountains and river plains have bisected three climactic subprovinces and encompassed nine geological types of shoreline formations. There have been sixteen distinct biotic communities and, by coincidence, an equal number of rare and endangered species ranging from the gray whale to the Santa Cruz long-toed salamander.

In a large part, the coastline is California itself since 85 per cent of the state's population is huddled within thirty miles of the ocean. The water's edge, whether fresh or salt, exerts a strong pull on the inhabitants and visitors to this state. By their large numbers, the people threaten to destroy the very resource they seek to enjoy and covet so avidly. Along the coastline, and elsewhere in this arid state, running or breaking water is treasured like white gold. But there still are places of great grandeur where solitude can be experienced although we have visited only a few in our journey along the coast.

For better or worse, but with a true overall magnificence, it all comes to an end at a pyramid-shaped monument marking the extreme southwest corner of the nation, at a rusty barbed-wire fence through whose gaps small Mexican boys wiggle to sell chewing gum. On the other side of the fence is the seaside resort area of Tijuana and that city's bullring. There are no trees on the low bluff rising above the gray sand beach sweeping south in a broad crescent from San Diego.

The Political Coast

Far out over the north Pacific a breeze springs up to ripple the surface of the gray ocean. This is where storms are born. The ripples are weak and directionless because the breeze keeps veering. They dash fitfully about, superimposed like small, criss-crossed gullies over the round-backed swells that have come from farther away but which were once ripples themselves. The breeze stiffens, and instead of continuing to veer, settles into a steadily increasing blow from the northwest. The ripples, changed to wavelets and then to full-born waves, grow steeper and tumble into whitecaps which begin to add energy to the longer-paced swells. With renewed vigor this force approaches the California coastline.

Reaching the narrow continental shelf, the swells are now traveling at 15 to 20 mph. The shallowing bottom organizes the swells into regular ranks. They are drawn up in an ancient battle plan, probably the most ancient—a combat in which one just sought to batter one's enemy into submission rather than to subvert him from behind. It is elemental and honorable. That is not to say that such tactics will win. There is a continual duel between the land and the sea. Near the beach the waves rear up, suddenly lose their fine-lined poise, and fling themselves with a quick burst of great strength against the shoreline. Their death is gentle, an almost inobtrusive sinking back into the ocean after balancing for a moment on the edge of land.

For ages this natural force has been the predominant factor in shaping the California coast. Along the central coast and most of the north coast, the waves are in the process of battering the headlands back. What little success they have had can be measured in the small pocket beaches between the rocky points where the residue has collected. Elsewhere, most notably along the sandy beaches of the south coast, the process has been further advanced. The longshore currents that carry the sand down the coast have become more dominant than the battering onshore swells. The coast has a more linear shape. It has been sandpapered smooth.

But there are two coastlines—the one shaped by these natural processes and the other more recently influenced by man.

A marina breakwater jutting into the ocean interrupts the natural flow of sand down the coast and starves beaches in the same way dams built on rivers trap the sediments that normally would flow to the ocean. Bulldozers slicing off mountaintops for subdivisions and freeways increase the sediment load and sudden rainstorms carry this beach-building material unhindered to the ocean. When houses built on the edge of the beach fall into the ocean because the protective sand has disappeared, it is because of what man has done unwittingly elsewhere. Or maybe the houses shouldn't have been built there in the first place.

Sewage wastes darken the waters and change the pattern of ocean life, creating marine deserts in some places. Offshore oil wells accidentally disgorge their contents, oil tankers collide, and the marine life is further altered. To seal off the mouth of an estuary means that it dies before its time and is no longer a refuge for migratory fish and birds or an intense breeding ground for life that circulates out into the ocean and up the food chain.

Then there is the aesthetics of jumbled power lines, high-rise apartments, neon lights, and in some places a Chinese wall of homes whose inelegant backs face the coastal highway. Along with the homes are the fences that block the public from the beaches. The coastal property owners complain they are being inundated by inland litter and fear that every sandaled foot is a legal threat to their land. They rarely mention the fact that they are hording a public asset, something that is increasingly thought of as California's most valuable natural resource. Everyone in the nation's most populous state wants a piece of the coastline. It is a modern-day gold rush.

I don't want to give the wrong impression. Overcrowding and the development syndrome do not prevail everywhere along the coastline. In fact, they are probably in the minority. The lyricism of a virtually untouched coast molded by natural forces still prevails, but it is the example of what has been poorly wrought in some places and the fear of what is yet to come that gave birth to what is now regarded as the "political coastline."

On a rainy January day in 1973 an unusual assemblage of people gathered in Room 4202 under the gilded dome of the state capitol in Sacramento. They were members of a state commission, to be sure, but they did not have the officious look of commission members. Maybe they would acquire it in time but at the present they seemed freer, less restricted to past solutions and previous governmental prejudices. They included lawyers, doctors, a magazine publisher, ranchers, housewives, a paving contractor, insurance agents, city councilmen, the owner of a fish company, marine biologists, university professors, and realtors. No blacks and only one noticeable Mexican-American were represented in the predominantly prosperous-looking group.

Sixty-five members were here out of a total of eighty-four, and they had come together in this legislative hearing room as the result of a remarkable political process. They were the members of six regional commissions and one statewide commission created by the passage of the Coastal Zone Conservation Act, an initiative measure put on the November 7, 1972, state ballot by conservationists to halt the hodgepodge development of the California coastline. The commission members had gathered for the first time to attend a briefing by state officials and by representatives of the legislature—a body which had failed to act on coastal-protection bills in its four previous sessions because of the strong opposition of large economic interests.

The issue of coastline protection had escalated to the number-one conservation cause in the state. Its opponents—large land developers, oil firms, and utility companies—spent a lot of time and money successfully defeating the passage of any legislation and mounting a campaign to defeat the initiative measure. By the time the voters got their first chance to express an opinion on the subject, the issue had developed into a classic confrontation between conservationists and large business interests.

In California, where the stakes always seem so big, national conservation organizations were pitted against development-minded firms with far-flung empires. Millions of dollars were spent to influence voters in one of those convulsive initiative campaigns that periodically stirs the populace up with emotionally charged arguments. In the short history of the national environment movement, perhaps no other issue was so extensively considered at the dual levels of a legislative body and a ballot box.

Curiously enough there was widespread agreement—at least lip service—to the idea that protection was needed for the coastline. Those who you might have suspected of being less than fully enthusiastic kept saying that local governments could do the job. Local governments, always very susceptible to pressures for increasing the tax base and oftentimes lacking in a larger viewpoint, hadn't done the job. The need for a higher, more responsive authority was clearly documented. On a personal level in many areas, all it took was a drive to the beach. Each person had his own experiences and was building up a backlog of grievances to spill out at the ballot box. It was mostly a subjective matter, but there were some facts.

The first statewide statistics on coastal ownership patterns were compiled in 1968 by the State Department of Parks and Recreation, and they showed that only about 90 miles of usable swimming beaches along the more than 1000-mile coastline were in public ownership. Later figures showed that of the total 1072 miles, 659 miles, or about 60 per cent of the coast, was in private ownership, and access to these areas was generally prohibited. The federal government owned 145 miles of shoreline with 100 miles of it—mostly in large military reservations—barred to the public. Most access was along the 263 miles, or 25 per cent, of the coastline that was controlled by cities, counties, and the state. The state tidelands, extending from the mean high-tide mark to three miles out to sea, are technically open to the public but difficulty is encountered when the beachgoer tries to get from his parked car to this wet sand area.

There were other problems besides the scarcity of recreation space. Estuaries and lagoons were clearly being lost as valuable wildlife habitats. In populous Orange County below Los Angeles, the board of supervisors favored giving Upper Newport Bay away in a land swap with the Irvine Co., a large land-development firm. The revolt against freeways had begun on the waterfront in San Francisco but spread throughout the state when the effect of future construction plans on the coast was determined.

A 1970 report by the State Resources Agency on power-plant siting require-ments showed that ten additional coastal sites would be needed in the next twenty years. A conservation group estimated that to meet the power requirements of the year 2000 a string of one thousand megawatt power plants would have to be spaced every six miles along the coast from Oregon to Mexico. This estimate turned out to be exaggerated but effective. The Santa Barbara oil spill of early 1969 gave visible dramatic evidence of the potential effect of that industry on the coastline. The re-sponsibility of managing the increasingly valuable coastal resource was fragmented among twelve state agencies and numerous other federal agencies and local govern-ments—the total number estimated at nearly two hundred—having an interest in the coastline.

The issue was ripe for something to be done. The question was: What and by whom? The final result—the commissions that exist today—did not evolve from the consensus of the legislative approach but rather from a default in the traditional processes. The powerful state agencies were opposed to such a measure because they were primarily interested in perpetuating themselves and preserving their bases of power. Such a new grouping could only erode their power to make highway, harbor, wildlife, parks, and planning decisions. Legislators listened to special interests with economic motives for keeping coastal management fragmented and ineffective, and they never acted. Governor Ronald Reagan—a firm believer in the local government approach—and his administration opposed strong statewide controls over the coastline but never offered any alternative course of action. And conservationists seemed politically naïve or more interested in their own ego trips than in saving the coastline. They did get the measure on the ballot but then almost blew the election because of internal dissension, lack of funds, and poor strategy. In the end, the voters came through, despite a complex web of arguments by the well-financed opposition throughout the media-dominated campaign.

As in most political campaigns, the expended verbiage had little to do with the issue at hand. Essentially, saving the coast was a motherhood issue, like seat belts in automobiles. It promoted itself and was hard to oppose. If you were against the initiative, you couldn't say "destroy our coast." The arguments had to be more complex and thus elusive.

The conservationists, including the well-organized Sierra Club, concentrated on stating that the measure would increase access to the beaches. This it would do, but only peripherally. The opposition claimed the act would decrease access and infringe mightily on private property rights, a possibility to be determined later by the courts. The primary issue that emerged was the veracity of the professional public-relations firm hired by development forces to oppose the measure. The "hired gun" image, promoted by conservationists and some powerful, sympathetic state legislators, did not help the development cause. The breakthrough for the conservationists in their muddled campaign came when their volunteer legal talent got the Federal Communications Commission to rule that television stations had to give them free time to match the opponents' well-financed advertising campaign. What resulted then was the unselling of the coastline.

The act, which passed by a substantial margin, clearly spelled out the goals to be followed by the commissions. "It is necessary to preserve the ecological balance of the coastal zone and prevent its further deterioration and destruction. It is the policy of the state to preserve, protect and where possible to restore the resources of the coastal zone for the enjoyment of the current and succeeding generations."

The commissions have the power to control development within one thousand yards of the water while they draw up a coastal land use plan for submission to the 1976 session of the legislature. For California, so growth minded in the past and a captive of the near-sacred doctrine of private property rights, even such a three-year pause to contemplate was clearly a revolutionary move.

There is one small place along the coastline, I won't say where it is, where a visitor can sit on a rock and feel surrounded by good, silent things. This does not mean there is no sound, because there is. But the sounds fit, one within the other. No sound or smell intrudes by itself, although it may seem separate for a short time. There is the rhythmic sound of surf, the scurrying of windblown sand, bushes, and grasses swaying, and the rush of wind about the ear.

Along with the sounds are the smells arising from the pungent warmth of the chaparral, the new green growth, the fertile decay of seaweed, and the moist salt air. The smells are all heavy, yet unobtrusive, because they too meld together. The sights are distracting because they seem to lead away from the essence. One sight is not enough, and the eye seeks more views when what has just been passed by may be all views. So I won't describe sights. Besides, this book is filled with pictures.

Now if the visitor sits long enough with his eyes closed in this one small place the inner rhythms start to match what is happening quietly outside. They never completely mesh because thoughts intrude (the mind is as impossible to control as the eye), but it is close enough for at least a little peace. As long as there is such a place, and fortunately along the California coastline there are many, people will keep coming to the edge of the land searching for something I prefer not to ever completely know, because if I did the essential mystery of something very beautiful would be lost. By comparison, political processes and the works of man seem insignificant. And this, fortunately, is the way it still is.